THE BOOK ON MEDITATION FOR LIGHT WORKERS

A Guide For Those On The Path To Personal And Planetary Ascension

Ka't Pleiadean Mandu

Cover Art by Dustin Matlock

Dedicated to all lightworkers, light warriors, starseeds, indigoes, crystals, golden children, rainbows, super psychics, blue rays, incarnated angels, wizards, walk-ins, fairies, gnomes, pixies, sprites, sylphs, undines and anyone else who feels that their calling is to serve humanity and anchor the light into Mother Gaia. I love you all more than words for your spirit and dedication to the peace of the planet and to Source Energy.

Table Of Contents

Foreword

Why I Wrote this Book

This book came about as a result of hearing the plights and difficulties of many of my beautiful lightworker friends who were having problems with meditation and its various aspects. On my Facebook page, I posed a question in order to determine exactly what was causing the most difficulty for light workers, in particular. This book sheds some light on ways that I personally had found to have worked for me over the years. Of course, these problems are not limited to light workers alone, but to any new meditator on the path to personal enlightenment.

What is a Lightworker?

The light worker is a traveler on the path to their personal ascension. They can be doctors, lawyers, shop assistants, car mechanics, or corporate executives. Most of them work toward it every day through meditation, fasting, watching what they eat, and often a vegetarian or a vegan diet is chosen. There is a feeling of having a grander purpose, that they have a mission to do something of significance for the planet and all thereon, through spreading love and light and anchoring positivity.

Characteristics of the Lightworker

They are often older souls who have lived many incarnations and learned many of life's lessons. With this knowledge, they have agreed to reincarnate as humans once again to help raise the planetary frequency and to help others reach enlightenment. They often feel misunderstood, lonely, left out. They follow the beat of their own drum, often to the despair of family and friends, especially while growing up.

They are not attached to material things because they know that life is more important. Some give their gifts of healing for free; many having taken vows of poverty in previous lives. They have memories of being on other planets and sometimes they want to go home because they don't fit in. They are protectors of life and animals, they hate violence and arguing because it shakes them to the core.

They are often dreamers and empaths and get caught up in the negative emotions of others, so regular escapes into nature are essential. Many have been witches, druids, kabbalists, shamans, wizards and others persecuted or misunderstood for their beliefs in previous lives, which they consciously remember.

They are the mystics of the modern world. They often have gifts and abilities carried over from past lives that they know they need but can't access just yet because the gifts are lying dormant within them through fear, due to persecution in past incarnations.

There are many different kinds of beings on a path like the one described above. There are the starseeds, who have connections with other star families, who have a far-away look in their eyes and look at the stars because they instinctively know that is their home.

There are incarnated angels, often, but not always, blonde, who are the ones that go out of their way to help someone, often at their own detriment.

Then, there are the elementals like fairies, the blue-haired dreadlocked people covered in mud because they spend so much time in nature, and there are others like gnomes, sylphs, and undines. And yes, they really can talk to trees!

The Lightworkers Mission

The light workers were one of the first waves of incarnated beings with assignments to help raise the planetary vibration and all thereon for ascension into the fifth dimension and beyond. There are light warriors and indigoes with their fiery spirits, then the more gentle crystals, rainbows, golden, and diamond children coming through, each generation retaining more and more cosmic memory.

So if you're reading this book, you are more than likely one of the above. However, for the purpose of this book and any that follow, I will be referring to all of the above under the heading of lightworker, for convenience sake.

So now that you've discovered that you're a lightworker, where do you start? Well, this is the thing. Many lightworkers start off floundering around, not really knowing how to get started. They know that they have a lot to give and they're usually way ahead on the kindness and compassion scale, but not always there in the development of psychic abilities. Many are born with these tendencies to a point but being a light worker demands much more than that.

Although it has become fairly mainstream over the last twenty years or so, thanks to the works of people like Doreen Virtue and Louise L. Hay, it is important to recognize that the path of the light worker is, first and foremost, a mystical path. That means years of disciplinary study, exercises, dedication and most of all, patience with self. As the famous wife of a rock star once said, 'it won't happen overnight, but it will happen.'

There are two key differences between the path of the light worker and that of the traditional practitioner of meditation. The first difference between the lightworker and those studying meditation, like within Buddhism, is that the focus of the light worker is more exoteric. That is to say that the lightworkers work is global as well as personal and, while other group are working toward global causes as well, there is no doubt that the light worker is probably a bit more gung-ho about it.

There's a sense of urgency in their natures, like time is of the essence, poised ready to charge on the command, sleeves rolled up ready to get their hands dirty and their hearts kicked around, waving their light sabers to free planet Earth and their fellow man. They really are a separate kettle of fish, which is why I have designed this book specifically for the needs and problems of lightworkers.

The second key difference is that lightworkers are co-creators with Source Energy. In order to manifest clearly, you need a clear, razor-sharp mind that is completely in your control.

Meditation, visualization and focus, and concentration will be dealt with in this book which should give you a good start toward manifesting the things you want as directed by your will, rather than what you don't want, that you are creating by default. It all starts with the ability to be able to meditate correctly, to be able to eliminate the negatives and reprogram the subconscious with positive thoughts that work for you, not against you.

It's a beautiful thing, the path of light, and for many of us it's what gets us up in the morning, our reason to breathe. However, it can take many around in circles of frustration, sometimes for years. So, I hope I can help take the frustration out of your experience and eliminate some trial and error by offering some semblance of a yellow brick road.

Chapter 1   What Is Meditation?

Meditation is the skill of letting go of all thought. You can say that it is the opposite of thinking. We run around in our busy day-to-day lives and we're thinking, thinking. In fact, if you said to the average Joe to stop thinking, he probably wouldn't know where to start, and he'd probably look at you as if you were crazy.

Our brains are constantly processing information, even when we sleep, but sometimes, just like a computer, our brains need a defragging. However, it is important to point out that your brain is not your mind. The brain is the physical component, the machine of the mind. If the brain is the car, then the mind is the driver.

Being the watcher of the mind

So, how do we let go of thoughts? Sound impossible at first; but, with consistent practice, the mind learns to submit to control just like when you establish any new habit, wanted or unwanted. In order to let go of thoughts, we have to watch the thoughts. We observe them, notice them.

Just like children jump up and down when seeking attention and then go on to something else when they have had their attention needs met, so, too, does thought. If you try to push thoughts away, they will still arise later. That's why so many people get stuck in a meditation rut because pushing thoughts away is a futile exercise.

Watching your thoughts arise without judgment means they can play out their energetic requirements and dissipate naturally, which will lead to the state of calm that we associate with meditation. This may take some time, maybe twenty to thirty minutes before the thoughts subside. The clearer you are, the less time it takes.

As a clearing of negative energies

Since we are not monks and are not locked up in some monastery, we encounter the trials and toils of others in our day-to-day lives. It may be hard enough to deal with our own problems, but when we're around others who are also having problems, for the lightworkers, who are often empaths as well, it can be difficult to let go of the energies impinged upon us.

Therefore, for the lightworker, it is imperative to clear yourselves daily and meditation is a really good way to do it. Once in a state of deep meditation, the mind can be cleansed of the day's negativity, like a mind bath. When the mind releases the effluvia of the day; so, too, does the aura, or astral energy body, which is what people perceive as your point of attraction, or your most dominant vibration.

Have you ever had someone say 'I love that person's energy' or 'I don't like their energy?" Have some people just made you want to be around them while others have just creeped you out and made the hair on the back of your neck stand up? It's the effect of the long-term state of a person's energy. So, keeping yourselves clear is tantamount to the evolutionary pace of the light worker; and, since you are the anchors of light, to the planet as well.

Separation of ego mind from Higher Mind

So, meditation is essentially the separation of the mind from itself. That is, the Mind, from the mind. Because of our Earthly incarnations in which we agreed to have a physical experience so that we could learn and become a greater part of Source Energy, or whatever you wish to call it, we were given the ego mind. The ego mind is not who we truly are, the Higher Mind is.

Of course, nothing is truly separated, but in our third dimensional world, it appears that way in our day-to-day lives. Trouble is, the ego mind has a personal agenda and is constantly on the go, creating and choosing what it wants and what it doesn't want. That's what it was created to do. But, sometimes it does it so well that the incessant chatter takes over from the Higher Mind to the point that we forget how to get in touch with it. Then, we start to feel alienated from Source and from others. Or, we believe false things about ourselves, like we're not good enough or we're too fat, too thin, too dumb...the list goes on. The Higher Mind doesn't believe any of those things because it knows that it is perfect.

So, standing back and getting some perspective on the state of the ego mind and observing it with the Higher Mind means you can get a sense of Who-You-Really-Are. Then, you are seeing through the Eyes of Source, which are your eyes.

So why meditate?

When we meditate, we close the door on the past and the future and stay poised in the now. This is where true reality lies, as the past has gone and is just a world of memories, some of them good, but a lot of them not so good. We find ourselves drifting off into a world that could have been and that is not all that productive to your day or to your emotional balance. The future is also not real, and although we may dream of a better life, some see their futures as bleak, to say the least, leading to anxiety, fear and stress.

For busy working mothers, meditation in the bath is a good way to get away from the kids and get a bit of peace. Light some candles and some incense and lock the door. For dads, meditation can be done while mowing the lawn or sanding a chair. Once you have your techniques under your belt, you don't have to find extra time to just sit cross-legged on the floor. I really enjoy meditating while I'm walking in the bush. With any of these activities described above, you are becoming relaxed and entranced in the task at hand, and so it is easy to slip into a state of No-Mind. This will be discussed in detail in Chapter 4.

For the lightworker, meditation is training the mental and spiritual matrixes to download and hold more light and energy, without side effects, and to refine and stabilise the higher light and crystalline bodies through the release of old ingrained negative energy patterns.

Ten Physical Benefits of Meditation

The benefits of meditation are too numerous to list in total, so I'll list ten from each life area.

The physical benefits are:
1. Your health improves. The calming nature of meditation reduces blood pressure and other stress-related illnesses.
2. Your breathing slows down and your oxygen intake improves.

3. More energy.
4. Better sleep.
5. Relaxes tense muscles, reduces headaches and migraines.
6. Balances DHEA and cortisol levels that contribute to weight   gain.
7. Slows the heart rate.
8. Brain function improves.
9. Increases the immune and endocrine systems.
10.   Slows the ageing process.

Ten Mental Benefits of Meditation

The mental benefits are:
1. Relaxes you so that petty matters no longer bother you.
2. Increases focus, discipline, concentration and willpower.
3. Memory and learning ability increase.
4. Improves relationships.
5. Self-confidence increases.
6. Reduces depression and morbid thinking.
7. You become a nicer, more tolerant ,and understanding person.
8. Helps you to see things without ego interfering.

9. Reduces the need for smoking, alcohol and drugs.
10.   Increased thought control and, hence, positive manifestation abilities.

Ten Spiritual Benefits of Meditation

The spiritual benefits are:
1. You feel more at one with all life.
2. Your capacity for love, compassion and all good emotions increases.
3. Ability to contact your angels and spirit guides increases through your improved connectedness.
4. ESP develops and/or improves.
5. You are happy and joyful for no apparent reason.
6. Your channelling abilities improve because you are clear.
7. You download higher and higher frequencies without issue.
8. Your life's mission becomes apparent.
9. Past life and inter-stellar memories become more frequent.
10.   Lucid dreaming and astral projection are normal for you.

So, now you have a clearer understanding of the necessity of meditation for the lightworker, and for anyone wanting a more satisfactory level of health and wellbeing in every way, we will now have a look at how to get started with your meditation practice.

Chapter 2   Getting Started

So, now you're ready to do a meditation session. That's awesome. A few things before you start. Make sure there are no physical distractions. Take the phone off the hook or put your mobile phone on vibrate and make sure you are not hungry. If you are, go eat something first and then wait half an hour while you digest. Go to the toilet. It's good to shower first, as this is a cleansing of the body ritual prior to the cleansing of the mind and spirit.

Choosing a Sacred Space

Find a place that is dry, airy and preferably insect free while you're starting out. Being an older chick, I like to sit with my back against a wall, cross-legged, either on my yoga mat, meditation cushion or on the bed. Make the space as sacred as you can so that the energies are kept clear by not using that area for any other purpose, if possible. Also, a small table or altar in front of you with a candle, incense, crystals, music or anything else that stimulates your higher consciousness is beneficial.

Getting Comfortable

Wear comfortable clothes, especially if you will be sitting in a cross-legged position. Baggy pants are best. Girls, from personal experience, I find it best to unhook your bras or take them off altogether. Guys, swap the jocks for boxers, tracksuit or yoga pant. Remove anything constrictive like rings or bracelets so the energies flow through the meridians freely. Tie your hair back so it doesn't fall in your face and take your shoes off. If the body isn't comfortable, the mind won't be either.

Sitting and Correct Posture

The ideal meditating position, in line with the traditions of the East, is to sit in the lotus position; that is, with both feet resting sole upwards on the opposite thigh. Of course, this is not mandatory; and, if you're like me and don't have rubber knees, you might be better off in a simple cross-legged position or even a sitting position...whatever is most comfortable for you. The most important thing is to keep you back perfectly straight for the entire time. Make sure you sit right up on top of the tailbone and let the other vertebrae rest on top. A meditation cushion will keep you upright and can prevent your getting pins-and-needles in your feet and legs.

Arms and hands should rest relaxed in your lap. Hands should be held in a simple mudra (see Chapter 7) to form a circuit of electricity within the body. You can cup your hands with the four fingers resting against the backs of each other, thumbs joining the first, or pointer finger.

Alternatively you can just have one hand cupped inside the other. Keep the shoulders relaxed. The head should not be looking directly out but at a slight angle to the floor, about thirty degrees. This stops you from being too alert, but not relaxed enough to fall asleep (hopefully). Eyes can be either closed, or almost closed. Keep the jaw nice and relaxed and hold the tip of the tongue up against the back of the top teeth.

Choosing A Meditation To Do

Simple Candle Meditation

Sitting in a meditation position:
1. Place a lighted candle in front of you at eye level.
2. Gaze into the candle for a few minutes.
3. Close your eyes and visualise the candle in your mind's eye for a few more minutes.
4. Repeat steps 2 and 3 for 10-15 minutes.
5. When you can visualise the candle in your mind without needing the candle itself, practice the visualisation without it.
6. If any thoughts enter your mind, don't worry, just let them come and go as they will without issue. Eventually they will stop. Maintain your position in the now.
7. After about a week, you can increase the meditation time as proficiency and time permit.

Simple Meditation On The Breath

Sitting in a meditation position observe the breath:

1. Focus on the rising and falling of the breath in the body. Watching and feeling the chest rising and falling can do this. Continue for five to fifteen minutes.

2. Another way is to watch and feel the air passing over the tip of the nose. Continue for five to fifteen minutes.

3. Another way is to count the breaths. Inhale for 3 and exhale for 5. Continue for five to fifteen minutes. This one is not a deep breathing exercise; however, as you get better at meditation, you can increase the counts for deep breathing. You can use the candle as a focal point for this if it helps.

   As with all breathing meditations, make sure there is no tension in the chest. Breathe through the nose only and NEVER suck air in through the mouth, unless you're doing pranayama yoga with a licensed instructor. Keep the neck, shoulders and chest relaxed throughout.

Watching the Mind Meditation

Sitting in a meditation position:
1. Go into a state of meditation until your mind is still.
2. See your mind as a beautiful clear still pond.
3. Watch any thoughts coming into it as if you were watching leaves blowing on the water.
4. Observe them, acknowledge them and watch them disappear. If they don't disappear that's ok.
5. When you get to a state where the thoughts don't come, sit there for as long as you can. You should feel a deep sense of peace in this place. If you don't get to this point, that's ok. It will come in time.

For those that are fairly new to the discipline of meditation, you might find frustrations arising. Just stay relaxed as getting frustrated defeats the purpose of achieving a sense of calm. Concentration in meditation is done in a calm and focused way, willing the attention back when it drifts off.

Just know that with regular practice it will all come together. In the next chapter we will look more closely at the things that can interfere with your meditative practice and how best to overcome them easily and quickly.

Chapter 3. Common Problems and Solutions

I will talk here about some of the most common causes of these problems in meditation and their possible solutions.

Resistance of the Ego Mind

The ego mind likes to do what it wants. It doesn't like being disciplined. If you try to make it keep still for any length of time, it will kick up a fuss. You have to train it, and that takes time. New meditators often get discouraged when they can't control the ego mind on the first attempt. Don't worry. It is not an easy task at first, even for the most seasoned meditators. However, like everything else, control comes with practice and distractions are less likely to bother you in time.

For the first few times, you will probably notice this resistance as drifting off after a few minutes, much like a child does when watching television. When the ads come on, they pay full attention because they are only thirty seconds long.

So your ego mind's attention may only be a few minutes and then it will say: This is boring. I want to do something else now.

A good meditation to get the ego mind in control is the white line of light meditation.

White Line Of Light Meditation

1. Close your eyes and see your mind as a blank, black screen. Watch the black screen; notice its clarity in its blackness. Running vertically down the centre of the black screen is a line of light, no thicker than a hair. Focus on the line of light.

2. When the ego gets restless, imagine a big broom sweeping the ego to the side of the screen. It will keep coming back, but you keep sweeping it away until it submits to your Higher Will. Keep bringing your attention back to the line of light.

3. Keep doing this until you can hold a black empty screen for a solid five minutes. Once you can do that you can dissolve

the line of light and just use the black screen. This will probably take a few sessions to accomplish, but it is well worth the exercise. For deep-insight meditations and for preparing yourself for channelling, you need to get the ego and all its subjective thoughts out of the way.

Ego is your own thoughts and your own spin on things. That is what we have to put aside. Meditation allows you to see things as they really are. You can observe that and notice new things, but you have to have your own personal ego thoughts in check. You have to get out of the way of the insights and messages that come to you. Otherwise, it's just you thinking, and that's not what meditation is about.

Frustration of Constant Thoughts

Unwanted thoughts can be extremely frustrating and this frustration can lead to annoyance, disappointment, despair and even anger. Your meditation time shouldn't be a time of anxiety. It should be a time of joy, healing and recharging the spiritual batteries. When thoughts arise, don't be hard on them and don't be hard on you. It's normal. Even the most experienced Zen monks had these problems when they started.

Take this opportunity to build patience and to use it as a patience meditation. That way, you are still building your spiritual discipline. You can even observe patience.

Be the watcher. Observe the thoughts. See yourself watching
what you're thinking without any judgment or feelings about the thoughts either way. Just watch like you're watching a show on television. Observe, acknowledge and let go. Don't nullify them because that just creates more resistance and perpetuates the problem. Just let them go when they're good and ready. Being neutral is key here. Detach yourself from the thoughts.

This is also a great opportunity to help you get into the now. Get a feeling of passing through the thought. Once the thought passes, you're in the now. Stay there for as long as you can.

Fidgeting

Fidgeting is another form of resistance. It is the ego mind coming up with an excuse to not be restrained, so it will make you think you are hungry, thirsty, hot, cold, uncomfortable, have to be somewhere else, wasting time, the list goes on. Of course, all of these are illusions and you should ignore these resistance mechanisms, especially if you prepared yourself and ate and drank before you started your session. Then, you know the ego is lying to you.

There is a story of a young monk who was told by his teacher to walk twenty paces from under the tree where they were in the direction the teacher gave and that would be where the young monk would do his meditation. He ended up on an ant's nest and he had to sit and meditate where he was, regardless of the circumstances. That's a disciplined ego mind!

So, when you want to fidget, fight the urge. Try to stay as still as you can for as long as you can, regardless of how you feel. You will be greatly rewarded with a disciplined and sharp mind.

Outside Distractions

The ego mind also likes to trick you into thinking that you can't meditate with all that outside ruckus going on...too much traffic, the party next door, someone walking through the house, people talking, laughing, phones ringing. You can meditate regardless of what is going on around you. Treat outside noises as you would your thoughts. Observe that they are there, acknowledge them and let them go to fade into the background.

The meditations for quickly getting into a state of No-Mind, to be described later, will help you to not be phased by outside noises. With practice, soon you will be meditating deeply anywhere, anytime, without any problem at all. Apart from that, you will also be able to induce a meditative state and still do your daily tasks.

Falling Asleep

This is a common one for beginners and is often caused by being a little too comfortable. If you like to meditate lying down or in a reclined position, or if you're sitting but you're not up on the tip of the spine, you are more likely to fall asleep.

One way to prevent falling asleep is to meditate with your eyes slightly open and just gaze at a spot on the floor or ground in front of you. That keeps the mind alert and aware and by doing that you are actually exercising your multi dimensional mind, because you are aware of what's around you but still observing the inner worlds.

Another way is to make your room a little cold, maybe turn the fan on. By making you just a little uncomfortable you are less likely to drift off.

Fear and Guilt

This is usually for people who have had strong religious upbringings that are against meditation practices. Because our core values are programmed within us before we turn five years old, they are sometimes harder to break. Just know that meditation has many benefits and that it is not against your God to do so. Freedom of the mind leads to spiritual liberation, which is the aim of meditation and any spiritual practice.

If fears and guilt persist, sometimes intervention like neurolinguistic programming (NLP) can help rewire the brain to a more favourable configuration for your purposes.

Also, affirmations work as well because you are essentially reprogramming your brain to eliminate chronic thoughts that no longer serve you. We will talk more about that later in the book when we discuss reprogramming meditations.

Now that we have outlined some of the common problems to meditation and given some solutions that will hopefully make your meditations more constructive, we will now look at getting and staying into the No-Mind state.

Chapter 4   Getting into No-Mind

Many new, and even experienced meditators often find the idea of getting into a state of no-mind one of the most difficult things to achieve in meditation. It is also largely the reason why many give up meditation, usually just when they are at the point of mastering the technique. It really isn't as hard as some people think.

Getting into no-mind means exactly that, no mind. That is, no mind as far as thought is concerned. You see, we are all so used to thinking continuously that many can't entertain the notion that it is possible for us to stop thinking. If they see that it may be possible, then they very often can't perceive that they can achieve it.

Have you ever had moments when you were a kid and you were in class, and the lesson was really boring? Suddenly you're looking out the window, drifting off in a trance, or staring into space until the teacher comes up to you and slams the desk, scaring the living bejeebus out of you?

You were in No-Mind.

Do you remember how peaceful it was, that there was no sense of anything, no time, no space, no rules, no one telling you what you should and shouldn't be doing? Just enjoy a sense of being. You can return to that state.

The Mist Meditation Technique

When I was working in the shopping centres doing psychic readings, one of my colleagues introduced me to this technique. It is great for busy people and for when you need to get centred for that meeting or interview and you can't find a quiet and peaceful place to meditate. You don't need to with this meditation, and it's just a great one for you to get into the no-mind state wherever you are.

Get into a comfortable position and start with observing the breath as you inhale and exhale. Feel how the mist goes into your chest and down into your lungs and out again the opposite way. Feel how it ebbs and flows. This is the balance of life. Observe it. Acknowledge the noise and chatter, traffic or anything else that's going on and just be aware that it is there.

When you have got into a steady flow, visualise yourself as having a hollow, transparent body, like glass.

As you breathe in, see the incoming breath as a coloured mist, any colour that resonates with you. As you inhale and exhale, see the mist flowing into your body at the feet, then rising to the knees, then the hips, torso, arms, neck and head.

When the body is saturated with your chosen coloured mist, centre your attention into the heart, so you are now sitting in the heart of your body.

Hold that there for a few minutes.

Then, visualise a golden pyramid hovering about ten centimetres (six inches) above your head.

Transfer your consciousness from the heart centre, rising up, to now be seated in the golden pyramid.

You should now find yourself in the No-Mind state. Hold it there for as long as you can without thought. Feel how it is just now, no past, and no future. Just now, and that's all there is.

If you wish to go into another meditation from there, you can. You will find it increasingly easy if you use the success memory of your meditation to get back into that state

Self Hypnosis Technique

Another way to get into a state of no-mind is through self-hypnosis. In order to reach a hypnotic state, start with a simple, full-body, relaxation technique.

A word of caution, self-hypnosis gets you directly into your subconscious; therefore, it is imperative that you are in a quiet place with no distractions. If not, any outside negative suggestion can take root in your subconscious and create problems down the track. Better to be safe than sorry.

While practicing this method for the first few times, it is best to lie down in a comfortable position.

Tense all of the muscles in your body as tense as you can for ten seconds. Then let everything relax. Starting with the toes, tell the toes to relax, then the feet. Feel them getting heavy. Feel the ankles relax and then the calf muscles. Feel the knees relax, the thighs and the buttocks relax.

Feel the lower back muscles relax. As everything relaxes, feel that they are weighing heavy and sinking into the mattress beneath you. Feel your internal organs relaxing... liver, kidney, spleen, uterus, stomach, pancreas, etc. Feel them all weighing like lead. Feel the spine relax, the ribcage, the heart, diaphragm and chest, relax. Feel your shoulders getting heavy and sinking into the bed. Feel your arms relaxing.

The upper arms, the elbows, the lower arms, hands and fingers are completely relaxed. Then, feel the neck relax, the muscles in your face, the forehead, the eyebrows, the eyes, the cheeks, the lips and chin. Feel the muscles in the head relax, scalp relax, your ears, your tongue, gums and jaw.

You should feel like you cannot move. Once in this state, repeat the following

Counting back from 5 to 1, 5, my eyelids are heavy.... 4, they're heavier still...3, I can barely keep them open any longer...2, my eyes are closed...and when I say 1, I will be in a deep state of meditation..........1.

As you practice this method, you will get quicker and quicker at it until you will relax within a few seconds and a state of deep meditation or no-mind will be attainable almost instantly, regardless of the surrounding environment.

When awakening, just say the following. Counting back from 5 to 1.....5, I am becoming more aware.....4, I am even more aware......3, I am beginning to wake up......2, I am fully conscious and when I count to 1, I will be awake, refreshed and full of energy (or ready to sleep if you are doing it before bed)...........1.

The self-hypnosis technique is excellent for reprogramming yourself for weeding out negative traits and replacing them with more love, more joy, more happiness, more abundance or whatever else you feel you would like to increase.

Pranic Breathing

Prana is pure life force. It is the energy that flows through all things. It is the stuff that holds the universe together.

Through watching and controlling the breath, we can reach the no-mind state. Most people breathe about ten to fifteen times a minute. Slowing down the breath ensures calm, peacefulness, and a longer life. The lightworker should aim to slow their breathing down to about four to six times per minute.

To start off, here is a simple breathing cycle of five just to give you the feel of it. There are generally four phases to a breath. Breathe in your own good time.

Breathing Exercise 1

Breathe in 1…. 2…3…4…5…
Hold the upper retention 1…. 2…3…4…5…
Breathe out 1…. 2…3…4…5…and

Hold the lower retention 1…2…3…4…5…
Repeat 10 times.

You may start to feel a little light-headed when doing deep breathing at first because your blood is learning to hold more oxygen. After a while, you will get used to it.

For attaining calmness, you can just slow down the breath with longer counts. They don't have to be even like the one above; in fact, it is more beneficial if the breathing out phase is at least twice as long as the breathing in phase.

There may be parts of the cycle that feel a little uncomfortable. If so, you don't have to do them. I personally find that if I breathe deeply, my lungs are full after three or four counts. So I extend the length of the upper retention to maybe six counts. As I don't have a problem with the breathing out phase or the lower retention phase I can still do a thirty second cycle with comfort. Find through trial and error what feels most comfortable for you.

Breathing Exercise 2

Here's one with a longer exhale phase. (fifteen seconds)

Breath in 1…2…3 hold 1…2…3
Breath out 1…2…3…4…5…6 and hold
1…2…3

Breathing Exercise 3

And finally (thirty seconds)

Breath in 1…2…3…4…5… hold 1…2 ...
3…4…5
Breath out
1…2…3…4…5…6…7…8…9…10…11…12…13…14…1
5
and hold 1…2…3…4…5…6…7…8…9…10

Now you're at thirty seconds or breathing twice a minute. That should be enough to calm down a charging rhinoceros!

If you notice, every time you get angry or upset, your heart rate goes up and your breathing gets faster. This feeds the emotional fuel and because you are in an emotional state physiologically, it's harder to stop the momentum of anger and rage.

The brain signals the fight or flight mechanism in the body, a primordial instinct triggered in the brain that has been there since caveman days. Extra blood starts to flow to the limbs, to the arms for fighting and throwing bottles and plates, and to the legs for fleeing. Plus, the adrenalin is in your muscles as well. So there is a lot going on in your body once you become angry.

If you can remember to calm the breath even just a little so that it doesn't trigger the physiological responses of anger...if you can catch yourself as the anger arises, you will be in control of the situation and a calmer outcome will be the result.

Meditation is the key to your developing this calm so that the rational mind prevails and you are in control, not your emotions.

Chapter 5   The Main Types of Meditation

Clearing Meditation

The clearing meditation is used, as the name implies, for clearing of negative or undesirable thoughts and energies. There are a few ways one can use the clearing meditation. Here is one way you might like.

Get yourself into a light state of meditation. Relax easy and enjoy being in the present moment. See a pale golden light entering your body and watch it swish throughout every cell in your body, like a gentle motion of a washing machine. Some of you may see a black effluvia coming out and loosening up out of your cells. This is karmic residue. Let it go. Continue until all karmic residue has disappeared.

Watch the mind and notice the things that are arising. They are coming up for clearing. Don't resist; just wash them out with the golden nectar of light.

This is a good one to do before you sleep to minimize the effects of negativity you have encountered in your day. By clearing them out as they come up, they don't get a chance to take hold of your psyche and you can make positive headway in clearing past karmic debt.

With each clearing meditation, you can reach deeper levels of karmic residue that may go back to previous lives. Clearing these old negative patterns will help you speed up your karma and things going on in your life, which may not have flowed easily, may now start to gain a positive momentum.

When I was younger, I used to have problems leading large groups of people. Even though I knew I could do it, I felt inadequate. In the early days of my meditation practice, I found that through clearing meditation, I started remembering a past life where I was a Chinese prince who led two thousand soldiers to their deaths against twenty thousand Mongols. I felt responsible for all those deaths. I had to forgive myself and clear the memory in order to move on.

Chakra Balancing Meditation

You can also focus on the chakras when doing clearing meditation. Chakras are the main energy centres in the spirit body. There are seven main chakras; but, new ones are opening up as we raise our vibratory levels. As we are reaching the fifth dimension of consciousness, the heart is becoming more and more the seat of the soul.

As a basic introduction, we will focus on the seven main chakras, but there are minor ones as well, one hundred and eight in total, sixty-six above the crown and forty-two below. As we evolve, the next set of chakras drop down into place.

Visualise each chakra in turn, spending about five minutes on each one. See it going from a murky colour, spinning and releasing any karmic residue, which usually looks like black or brown goo. Spin it out and see it leaving the chakra. When you can see it growing back to the size of a dinner plate and the colour is bright and clear, move on to the next one.

Sometimes the chakra is abnormally big. That's not necessarily a good thing. Best to get it into alignment with the others so the energies can flow freely between each chakra.

First - The Base Chakra – Red

The Base Chakra is where we have our view of self and of our world. It is the realm of survival, security and all primal instincts. Situated at the base of the spine, it is red in colour.

Traits of a healthy, balanced base chakra are confidence, vitality, honesty, strength, outgoingness, and standing your ground.

Second - The Sacral Chakra – Orange

The sacral Chakra is where our self-respect, success and self-expansion reside. It is the realm of your zest for life and joyfulness. Being emotional, it relates to sensual pleasures.
When unbalanced, you feel inadequate and stressed due to responsibilities. It is situated at the navel.

Traits of a healthy, balanced sacral chakra are sexual fulfilment, independence, enthusiasm and happiness in where you are right now.

Third - The Solar Plexus Chakra – Yellow

The solar plexus chakra is where our self-esteem and clarity of vision resides. It's where we get our 'gut' feelings and is situated at the diaphragm, in between the rib cage.

Traits of a healthy balanced solar plexus chakra are optimism, positivity, fun, laughter, self-confidence.

Fourth - The Heart Chakra – Green

The heart chakra is where our ability and depth of love resides. It is also compassion, self-control, and understanding. It is situated in the middle of the chest.

Traits of a healthy, balanced heart chakra are sympathy, empathy, and unconditional love for and nurturing of others and self, and giving with no desire for anything in return.

Fifth – The Throat Chakra – Blue

The throat chakra is where we communicate how we see our world. It is here that we convey what we know and our need to be heard. It is situated at the throat at the Adam's apple.

Traits of a healthy, balanced throat chakra are speaking one's truth in a positive manner, respect, and self-expression.

Sixth – The Third Eye Chakra – Indigo

The third eye chakra is where we experience our intuition. Because it is the realm of the pineal gland, it holds our spiritual experiences and visions. It is situated between the eyebrows.

Traits of a healthy, balanced third eye chakra are idealism, altruism, desire to serve humanity, and helping on a global level. The wave of indigo children that incarnated in recent years are here to help the downtrodden and make a difference to the planet.

Seventh – The Crown Chakra – Violet

The crown chakra is where our inspirations and epiphanies come from. It is our direct telephone line to Spirit. It is situated at the top of the head.

Traits of a healthy, balanced crown chakra are creativity, art, vision, and idealism...wanting to create a better world.

When doing chakra meditation, systematically go through each one for about five minutes, seeing the negativity spinning out of it and growing to about the size of a dinner plate, glowing healthy, and a clear colour.

The Reprogramming Meditation

Once we have cleared some of the negativity out with our clearing meditation, we can work on imbuing the positive qualities that we wish to increase through meditating on those qualities.

By meditating on more of these things like love, compassion, joy, and health, we increase our attraction to those things within ourselves. As a result, we bring more of those things into our lives. This creates a positive momentum of attracting more and more of these things while you download more and more until it becomes unstoppable. That is when you don't have to think about behaving in a particular way. It has become second nature to you.

I would recommend reprogramming in the morning for half an hour and then clearing in the evening for half an hour before bed, increasing as you wish and as time permits. You could also do a mixture of clearing and reprogramming before bed so that the new positive thoughts get to take root during the night while you're asleep.

Use of Affirmations in Reprogramming

Affirmations are a brilliant way of reprogramming the unconscious mind. However, many people have done them for years only to be dismayed and disillusioned by their lack of success.

The reason why success has taken so long is because they usually haven't done a clearing meditation first. You wouldn't plant a new crop without taking out the remains of the old crop. So similarly, a new crop of positive thought affirmations are not going to be tilled in healthy soil while the leftovers of past thoughts still remain.

As these thoughts have been there for so long, more than likely for most of your life, the roots are strong and stubborn. New shoots will hardly have a chance to take a firm hold. You have to weed them out aggressively...out of the garden of your mind, with no mercy and no attachment.

Our black and white mirror exercise will reveal those areas which no longer serve you, and where you can use a new positive thought that brings good into your life. Usually, when you strip your conscious back to the bare bones, it comes down to your not feeling good enough in some way, shape, or form.

These are things we encountered in childhood, a scolding, taunting on the playground, an angry priest or minister. Somehow, we have hung on to that thought and made it true. It isn't. It never was.

Affirmations need to be written in a positive manner. Don't write: "I'm never going to be negative again." It contains two negative words that you're affirming, never and negative. Rephrase it to say: "I am always positive."

Many new age writers have masses of information on the science of positive affirmation work. Dale Carnegie, Norman Vincent Peale, and the queen of positive thinking, Louise L. Hay, are all worth reading. However, you must remove your unconscious weeds regularly with clearing meditation to get faster and more beneficial results.

I love to use "I love and approve of myself" and I might say it three hundred times a day for about a week if I'm feeling particularly vulnerable. You can say it really fast and you can say it silently or whisper it as you're walking down the street or on the bus going to work or school. Louise's book, <u>You Can Heal Your Life</u> ,is brilliant for alleviating the negative thoughts that cause illness.

Problem solving Meditation (Contemplation)

Contemplation is the act of looking at a situation and trying to understand it. When contemplating, it is best to approach the subject with curiosity. When we look at something with curiosity, we take the subjective feelings out of it. Even if it is something that we don't like, for instance a bill or an adverse situation, look at it for what it is. Don't put you fears, opinions, likes, and aversions onto it. It is just a thing. Nothing more. See it for its emptiness. It is good to use contemplation when solving problems, but first, let's do an exercise.

Contemplation Exercise 1.

Find an object of some kind, anything at all. If you're outside, you can find a rock or a stick.

Relax and go into a light state of meditation. Now, open your eyes slightly and ponder the object, let's say it's a rock. Ponder the rock. Turn it around and examine every atom of it. Look for information, any telltale signs of where it might have been. Feel the nature of the rock, feel its atoms. Ponder on how old it is, what it may have seen in its life. Did it see the dinosaurs? Was it a part of a bigger rock? Really examine it and let the thoughts flow into your mind. The rock has a recorded history energy grid. Try to tap into it. Connect with the rock, be the rock. It is only by becoming the rock that can we fully understand the rock. Imagine what it would be like to be the rock. What sorts of insects were crawling over it? Isn't the rock magnificent in its creation? It's atomic structure? Is the rock totally unique or are there other rocks the same?

You get the idea?

When you get the hang of contemplating on a physical object, you can contemplate on a problem that's bothering you. Turn it over and see every angle. Dig into every nook and cranny; see all of its perspectives. If the problem is with another person, see how they think. Imagine what it is like to be them and to have been brought up by their parents in their situation. See why they have formulated the views that they have.

Contemplation Exercise 2.

.

Go into a light state of meditation.

Take a problem that has been troubling you and look at the problem head on. Observe how the problem makes you feel.

Notice that you don't wish to feel bad.
Ask yourself, what is the worst case scenario?
Can I adjust to that?
What would it mean if it came to that?
Would I survive?
Would it kill me?
Is it really all that bad?
Have I overcome this problem in the past?
If so, then I can do it again because I have already achieved success in overcoming this problem.

Keep asking yourself questions to gain more insight and notice what comes up. Look at all the sides if others are involved.

Sometimes I like to do this contemplation meditation as I type. That way I can remember the internal dialogue I had with my Higher Self and look back over it for clarity.

Contemplation as a problem-solving meditation can be extremely rewarding. It can almost make you love your problems because they are so much fun to solve. Like anything else, the more often you do it, the better you get at doing it.

Once you have found a solution, implement it. The lightworker needs to travel light; so, getting rid of as much baggage as possible is essential if you're to help others, especially if you're doing energy healing work. When doing reiki, you don't want to be putting your "stuff" onto others who have come to you for help.

The Use Of Visualization For Manifestation

Visualization is one of the most important components of the lightworkers work. We are co-creators with Source to build a new and beautiful world; therefore, we must be powerful manifesters. However, you can't manifest unless you can meditate correctly, at least you can't manifest deliberately. You can manifest by default; we do that all the time. Most of the time, we manifest things we don't want.

The key to manifestation is being so clear and sure of what we want that we can't stop thinking about it. The daydreams you have about the desired situation strengthen its presence in thought form in the non-physical realm.

There are four stages of manifestation that correspond to the Four Worlds. These are

Thought	Spiritual World
Ideation	Mental World
Creation	Astral World and
Manifestation	Physical World

If any of these stages are not present, your manifestation will not occur. Instant (or very quick) manifestations occur when all four of these realms are occurring simultaneously on multidimensional levels. Advanced kabbalistic techniques use this method to control the elements and other things. See the work of Franz Bardon for more on this topic.

One of the best exercises I have used since I started thirty years ago is the color visualization exercise. In order to be successful at building up your color visualization, you have to learn to concentrate.

We focus on the task at hand, learning color visualization for the bountiful reward of being the master of our own manifested destiny. That's focus.

Concentration is how we go about that task, and how we go about it is to look at the color.

Color Visualization Exercise (Focus And Concentration)

Go into a light state of meditation.

Open you eyes and take the object with the color that you wish to visualize. Look at it and think of nothing else. See nothing but the color. Feel yourself being immersed in the color. Do this for 30 seconds to a minute. Then, close your eyes and visualize the color exactly and clearly in your mind's eye.

When visualizing it, see yourself in your meditation space surrounded by the color that fills the room in a dense mist. Repeat for 5 to 10 minutes a day until you can feel that you can recall that color with absolute clarity at will. Usually, this takes about a week. Then, go on to the next color and the next.

Soon, with persistent practice, you will be a master visualizer and, in turn, a master manifester.

Psychic Attack

Many of my lightworker friends and colleagues have had an ongoing battle with psychic attack. People with malefic intent who direct harm to others because they don't share the same beliefs as the lightworkers do this. The sad part is, they really believe they're doing good, and they do it, 'in the name of (add deity here)' which they follow. They are very often family members or close friends. Of late, they are people on social media pages who make it their mission to send out malefic intent to others.

The trick is, at the end of the day, good people offer good intent. If your intentions are pure, it doesn't matter how you got there, you are a good person and that's all that matters. Source Energy recognizes this, have no doubt, and those who attack others in Source's name, are not the kind of people Source wants to have around. Just because you're a lightworker, doesn't mean you have to be a pushover. To protect yourselves from these poisonous barbs, here is a protection meditation.

Just as a note, some people like to cut off the negative energy tentacles and send the energy back as love. You can do that if you wish. If you do decide to do it that way, make sure you draw down the energy from Source, through the crown chakra. Otherwise you will get very drained, very quickly, which is what your attackers are hoping for.

Psychic Attack Meditation For Protection (Auric Shell Hardening)

Go into a light state of meditation.

Visualize your aura as an egg shaped energy field around your body.
If you have been psychically attacked, you will see grey energy tentacles leeching on to your chakras. These are the malefic energies of your attackers.
If you see them, visualize a large sword cutting all of these tentacles at the chakras. Cut all around the body and especially under the feet and top of the head. You can use Archangel Michael if you wish. (You should also do this physically with a knife).

When you have cut all of the tentacles, seal your aura.

Visualize blue light bombarding your aura in vast amounts. See it concentrating in a fine crust on the outer perimeter of your energy field. See the light thickening this crust to about three inches (5 centimeters) thick. Continue until you feel you have enough protection.

Go about your daily business.

You can add white or golden light to this if your wish.

Chapter 6   Mantras

What Is a Mantra?

In every religious tradition, the beginning of all things created by Source was from the Word, the Logos. The bible says: "In the beginning was the Word. And the Word was with God and the Word WAS God."

The act of speaking creates a physical reality. That is why it is so important to think before we speak because with every word, and as co-creators with Source, we are creating our own reality …every minute of every day, with every word we utter.

How Do Mantras Work?

Words have power. Words that are mantras have been uttered for thousands of years and have the positive intent of millions of people that have said them before you. They have phenomenal, mind-blowing power! You're literally riding on their spiritual coat tails to fast track your manifestations.

When you utter a mantra with intent, you are putting your own name on it and all of that momentum, those millions of mantras spoken before you, now comes to you. However, you have to be mindful and not misuse them.

Not just any words can be used as a mantra. They have to be old words that are anchored in the vastness of eternal consciousness. Names of deities, widely used mantras like AUM are best.

They can be spoken, or sung, or breathed, or thought. Writing them down works really well, too, as it imprints on the subconscious in a way similar to that of affirmations.

In meditation, the mantra, when repeated for some time, starts to change your vibratory rate, raising it to be one with the mantra itself.

Mantras can also be used to dislodge old negative thought patterns that are manifesting in the physical body. For lightworkers who are doing reiki or other energy healing work, the use of mantras can enhance your results dramatically as it aids in the transfer of prana or healing energy.

Mantras For Chakra Clearing

Mantras work extremely well with chakra meditation and each chakra has its own corresponding mantra. These are seed mantras, which don't have a direct translation but are extremely powerful.

They are as follows:

1. The Root Chakra Mantra is LAM. Use this to clear and balance this chakra. LAM will also help in developing clairolfaction (astral scent)

2. The Sacral Chakra Mantra is VAM. Use it to clear and balance this chakra. VAM will help with the development of clairgustation (astral taste)

3. The Solar Plexus Chakra Mantra is RAM. Use it to clear and balance this chakra. RAM will aid in the development of clairvoyance (astral sight)

4. The Heart Chakra Mantra is YAM. Use it to balance this chakra. YAM can be used to develop clairtactility (astral touch)

5. The Throat Chakra Mantra is HAM. Use it to balance this chakra. HAM will aid in the development of clairaudience (astral hearing)

6. The Third Eye Chakra Mantra is AUM. Use it to clear this chakra. HAM will help to develop your clairsentience (astral knowingness)

7. The Crown Chakra Mantra is Silence. Focusing on No-Sound will help clear this chakra.

Some meditators like to use the sound NG on the Crown chakra. Use it if it resonates with you.

Physical Benefits of reciting mantras

Mantras have been recognized by the medical profession to normalize DHEA levels and brain wave patterns, and lower blood pressure and cholesterol, and to help cure insomnia.

There are many kinds of mantras. I would recommend that you try both the eastern mantras and the western affirmations. The latter are ones you can do around the house. If you don't have time to sit and do a reprogramming meditation after your clearing, you can do them at any time during the day.

Chapter 7 Mudras

We can't finish off a book on meditation without examining the use of the mudra and its role. After all, it's what we do with our hands, right?

Well actually it's far more involved than just putting your hands and fingers together to form a shape. Mudras form electrical circuits in the body and are very beneficial to health and vitality.

How do mudras work?

Each of the five fingers represents an element. When a finger is in contact with the thumb, it brings healing to that region of the body.

The elements represented by the fingers are as follows:

Index finger is air
Middle finger is ether
Ring finger is earth
Little finger is water and
The Thumb is fire.

Some of the best known mudras are the ones seen on Buddhist statues or the ones that people tend to do spontaneously. One of the most common is joining the thumb and the index finger and resting the backs of the hands on the knees while sitting in the lotus or cross-legged position.

Another is joining the tips of all the fingers together. This is a popular one used for channeling as it forms a strong circuit within the body so that energy is focused on the entity being channeled.
I will talk more about channeling in future eBooks.

In order to get the most out of mudras, they need to be done with both hands for a period of time. This is why it is beneficial to use them during meditation, provided you are meditating longer than about twenty minutes.

Here are some examples of mudras and their benefits.

Mudras For The Chakras

To open the Root Chakra touch the tips of the thumb and the index finger, keeping the other three fingers rounded.

To open the Sacral Chakra place the right hand on top of the left hand resting in the lap, tips of the thumbs touching, so that it resembles a bowl.

To open the Solar Plexus Chakra place your hands in front of your stomach, joined as if you were praying but the tips pointing away from you. Do not put the palms together, just the fingers and cross the thumbs.

To open the heart chakra place the thumb and the index fingers together as in the base chakra position, except the right hand is in front of the heart, the two fingers at the heart and the left hand is on the left knee.

To open the throat chakra, place the hands in a similar bowl position to the sacral chakra position, only lift the thumbs up so as to form a circle rather than a bowl. This resembles the open throat.

To open the third eye chakra, place hands in front of the chest. The middle fingers are straight and touching at the tips, pointing away from the body. The others are bent at the second knuckle. The tips of the thumbs are touching. So it looks like a heart shape with a steeple on top.

Lastly, to open the crown chakra, place your hands in front of your stomach and interlock the fingers. Only the ring fingers are pointing straight up and joined at the tips. The thumbs are crossed right over left.

Some others you might find helpful

If you're feeling sad

Join the tips of the thumbs with the index finger, keeping the other fingers straight. This works on the air factors of the body: intellect, disposition, and mood. It brings happiness and joy and improves memory.

If you're feeling tired

Joining the tips of the thumb with the tips of the ring finger and small finger and keep the other fingers straight. It helps with getting prana into the body.

For weight loss

Tip of the ring finger at the base of the thumb. This is held on a pressure point that helps in speeding up the metabolism.

There are far more mudras than I could possibly cover here, so hopefully this will give you a taste of what you can examine in more depth. There are fantastic resources both online and in print with hundreds of illustrations. So, go knock yourselves out.

Chapter 8 Global Meditations for Lightworkers

The Golden Age

The lightworkers mission is to bring the Golden Age into manifestation on Earth. By a Golden Age, we mean a world where there is peace...one where corruption, war and famine are non-existent...one where people care about people and help them freely with no expectations in return. The "What's In It For Me" mentality is gone. People are free to worship whom or what they wish without fear of retribution. As Audrey Hepburn once sang "Ahh, wouldn't it be lovely?"

I think most of us dream of a beautiful world as described above at some time or another, but sometimes we get so caught up in our day-to-day trivial issues that solving the problems of the world seem out of our reach. The truth is, it isn't really. We just have to develop the things we want in the world within ourselves, and our smaller communities first. World peace really does begin at home, in YOUR home.

Meditation for World Peace

This meditation, like all the global meditations to follow, will start with a personal component and then work outwards.

Go into a light state of meditation. Visualize a soft golden light flowing down from the heart of Source, down a tube through all of your upper chakras. See it entering your body and your aura through the crown chakra. Feel it flowing down through all of your chakras and out through the base chakra, through the Earth Star portal chakra and anchoring down into the iron core heart of Mother Earth (Gaia). Continue to see the golden light pouring through you until your aura is completely filled and saturated with a soft golden light. Hold that for a moment.

Start to feel that this light is peace itself. Feel the comfort from your Source as it washes away all worries and concerns. Know that there is nothing that can defeat you in the long run, and that all problems are transient. All fear-based feelings subside as you rest in the knowledge that everything is taken care of, that there is an invisible hand that never lets you down, and that you are always connected, even when you think you aren't. Know that every need is taken care of.

See yourself as a warrior of peace, standing your ground and deflecting any adversity that comes your way. See your light shield as you hold it up, averting any negative person, word or circumstance. Stay centered in your peace and do not be moved. If you feel anger arising, say to Source,"Is that it? Is that my test? Do you expect me to crumble? Is that your best shot?" See yourself immovable and impervious to being rattled or shaken by outside people or conditions.

When you have reached a sense of staying centered no matter what is going on around you, you are ready to project that into Mother Earth.

See everyone on Earth getting everything they want out of life. See them happy and healthy. See the faces of people smiling and notice how it makes you smile with love and joy. Feel the Earth smiling also, for she is happy. See people bartering and that everyone has enough, whether it be money or not, see all business transactions conducted from the heart. Notice how the business executives are feeling joyful that they have been able to aid in such a significant way. See them feeling far more rewarded than abundant wealth at the expense of others, as it was in the old world system. See everyone living life in peace. Imagine!

Hold this state of peace for as long as you can, at least ten to fifteen minutes. Remember to draw down the light from Source and through the crown chakra. If you emanate your own personal energy out into the world and don't keep the infinite flow of Source going, you will become drained and tired. Pulling down the light from above gives you an unlimited supply of all good things that you want to embody in yourself and in the world.

When you establish peace within yourself, you anchor it within yourself, and it becomes a part of your vibration, thus raising it. The more you do it, the more light you bring down, the more you become the embodiment of peace for yourself and for others. That is the work of the true lightworker.

You can repeat the above to embody love, compassion, joy, abundance and anything else that you would like. Remember to fill yourselves up first because then, and only then, can you overflow and radiate these qualities out into the world.

Chapter 9. Conclusion

As a final note, I just want to thank you for reading my book. It is a simple guideline and hopefully it will fuel the fires of you looking into meditation further. It is important to be proficient in meditation to be able to work on other planes of existence for planetary healing and growth.

Tips and Resources

I would recommend you to do some of the guided meditations if you're starting out, or even if you're not. They are very good value for helping you to keep focused. There are some excellent ones on www.youtube.com. Also, there is a wide range of meditation music available and they are in different time durations, so that when you feel you would like to meditate longer, there is something there that you can use if you like meditation music. Some people prefer silence. Do whatever is easier for you. There is no right or wrong way, as long as you get comfortable and in tune.

I would also recommend the binaural beat meditation music as well. These have theta or delta waves embedded into the track, which can help you attain a deeper meditation.

Once you get into the routine of meditation, you won't want to go a day without it. If you want, join a meditation class that helps you to discipline yourself. There are many meditation retreats being offered at yoga and Buddhist centers around the globe. Some of them accept payment by donation that includes accommodation, like the Vipassana Centers. This is a beautiful thing that they are providing in service to others. Vipassana meditation is insight meditation. It focuses on self-observation to overcome suffering.

So go check out the plethora of information available and don't forget your own insights that you will gain through your increased meditation.

A special thank you to Dustin Matlock for the cover art, Morgan Houghton, Susan Cerato and Shar for the proof reading, and all of my friends and supporters in the light. Without you I would have no reason to write this.

Enjoy and be blessed as you travel on this profound and wonderful journey.

Love and light always.

35300322R00049

Made in the USA
Lexington, KY
05 September 2014